Aye yes, the tears of Mama Africa that absolutely no one sees, can grasp, or talk about. It's June 1, 2021, and already I have to interrupt this book to what I saw vision wise and dream wise. So, before I get into this book, of AFRICAN – BLACK PEOPLE CUSS OUT, let me tell you my dreams as well as, vision.

Yes, it's early morning. Before 7am, and I should have been writing long ago but did not get up to write. Sleep was great but daunting. Laying there in bed not too long ago with eyes closed, the face of the Reggae Artist D'Angel appeared before me. <u>She was smiling,</u> and all of a sudden; this creamy light appeared around her from her head going down. The shape of the creamy light around her was in the shape of a triangle that you would see on the roof of a house. You know what. Let me stick an icon of a house for you to see the shape I am talking about.

That triangle was the shape of the light that outlined D'Angel from her head down. And I am so not going to analyze this light or shape because visions I truly cannot pinpoint. I truly do not know what that shape and light represent so, I am leaving things alone. Listen, for me, and what I know. D'Angel represent the DEATH ANGEL. <u>BLACK FEMALE DEATH.</u> So, I do not know if Female Black Death is telling me in her way <u>that;</u> <u>for a surety, she is going to sink a land somewhere soon.</u> And I am going to leave it at that. You will not comprehend me seeing D'Angel in this way, but I know.

As for my dreams, this one particular dream I could not get away from. My dream world would not let me let go of it therefore, the dream kept coming up in my dream world.

Dreamt, <u>LAVA.</u> The lava was flowing like a river and this female reporter in a helicopter was covering the story and telling people about the lava as well as, showing them the footage. However, you could not see the helicopter or the Female White Reporter that was covering the news; story. You will not comprehend not seeing the helicopter or the White Female Reporter, but in my dream world, you do not have to see people or things to know the colour of the person or object. Therefore, I do not need eyes to see certain things, I just know. Yes, you will not comprehend this, and this is fine. It's like some spirits you cannot see but you know they are there, can feel them. And, I don't think that's a good explanation on my part therefore, let me get back to my dream.

Seeing the Lava flowing like a river, <u>IT WAS IMPLIED THAT THE LAVA FLOWING WAS IN INDIA AS WELL AS, CANADA.</u> Des Carte and or, Des Camp. No, I am sure Des Carte. I do not know if it's a region or place in Canada and or, what Des Carte represent and or, mean if it's Quebec. Seeing the Lava Flowing in my dream, knowing the implied target, and Des Carte, I did now want to see anymore so I quickly woke up out of my sleep.

Did the dream keep playing in my head?

Yes

Going to the washroom and going back to sleep, I could not get away from this dream. I kept dreaming about Lava. So yes, Earth is going to continue to burn. Well, I told you in another book

Earth is going to burn. This I know for a fact without doubt. Plus, I did tell you in another book about the burning smell I had when it came to Canada therefore, I did not know which province was going to burn.

I will not analyze this dream. It is self explanatory. Canada just have to stay focused. And with God wanting me to plant a seed in Canada, it does not mean that Canada will not escape destruction. Canada has and have been doing things that are not right in the eyes; sight of God therefore, the different heads of state from their Civil Leaders, Provincial Leaders, Federal Leaders are being held accountable spiritually for their actions. Humans are being judged; well, have been judged. The White Race will not go unpunished for their ills; all the ills they've done here on Earth. Canada is no exception. Canada too must pay and pay dearly for the wrongs of its people especially, the wrongs of their government officials no matter the jurisdiction. And I am going to leave things as is.

So, Provinces like Quebec, Alberta, British Columbia should be on the alert in my view. I don't know if my thinking is right for some. When the dry season truly hits, just send up a water plane and just drop some water on the area's prone to fires. Hey, think ahead. Yes, cost, but who knows.

India I will not touch because I truly do not know the land. Babylonian Death is truly different. I did not see any Babylonians in my dream therefore, I cannot tell you of a death toll if any. I just have to watch and see like you.

My other dream had to do with water and flooding. It was as if this land sank. I cannot tell you which land sank, but a land is going to literally sink. When, I truly do not know. Which land I truly do not know.

Death do mask death for me at times. When Death do not want me to know so that I cannot warn a land, DEATH DO MASK DEATH FOR ME.

So yes, a land is going to sink somewhere, and I do not know if this is the reason why I saw D'Angel — Black Female Death.

My other dream had to do with Lava. Like I said, I could not get away from this; Lava in my dream world. What was odd for me with this Lava Dream was the small and or, young White Child; girl no more than 6 or 7 that I saw. She was showing me things; yes, Lava. I can't remember if she was talking to me. So no, I do not know if Young White Children are going to die but something is truly not right somewhere, and I am so going to leave this dream alone. Hell is going to be on land. NO, HELL HAS AND HAVE COME DOWN TO EARTH LITERALLY and humans have no one to blame but humans; self.

My other dream had to do with Black People. I truly do not know if this is going to be a global thing, BUT A LOT MORE BLACK PEOPLE ARE GOING TO DIE. Oh God, just seeing Black Men laying face down in Black is truly not a good sight for me. It is truly disturbing and painful. So yes, the Death Toll for Blacks is going to rise exponentially from the looks of it.

Did I dream about family members?

Yes, but I cannot worry about my Jamaican Family back home, or my family here in Canada. I am not the only one in my family with sight. Therefore, I am hoping that those who have sight and care about their sight will rely on it. Yes, their sight is truly not like mine. I can see further than them, see the past, present, and future, connect and communicate with all around me including the different Levels of Death, and I am going to leave it at that.

Tyler Perry. I know I dreamt about him, but I so cannot remember the dream. I do not know if something is wrong with him. You know what, let me leave things alone because; <u>THE DEVIL KNOW WHAT HE'S DOING.</u> Therefore, Black Americans truly need to look into self literally and for real and wake up. They are truly not safe in the land they are in. And I will say this again in this book.

<u>"GET OUT."</u>

STOP SEEKING JUSTICE IN AN UNJUST LAND. DEATH OWN AMERICA THUS, YOUR <u>"WHITE HOUSE."</u> Figure it out if you can.

So, now that you know and are up to date with my vision and dreams. If you can help, help by letting the lands know of what I see. There is only so much that I can do. And don't you dare say. Well, they are only dreams. And all I have to say is, wow to the amount of them that has and has come to fruition. You are just not reading and seeing. Dreams are my way of telling you and showing you what is to come; is going to happen.

So, truly do your part if you can and lend a helping hand. And yes, there are more dreams in this book. Continue reading. I just needed to let you know of what I saw now; this morning June 1, 2021 because; it is <u>HELL HERE ON EARTH ALL AROUND.</u>

<u>*ONWARDS I GO WITH THIS BOOK.*</u>

What do you think of God?

Do you think God can sin?

Do you think God would bow down to Death?

Do you think God created Death?
Do you think God is Death?

What do you truly think and more?

As I look at life, I have to think of the truth of God, and I cannot let others, or other nations take the TRUTH OF GOD FROM ME.

I cannot buy into the lies of the Churches no matter the denomination of that Church whether; Protestant, Islamic, Roman Catholic, Church of God, Mormon; whatever.

I cannot buy into the lies of the clergy no matter the denomination whether you are; a Priest, Deacon, Preacher, Imam, Rabbi, and more.

My life is precious with God, and <u>I CANNOT LET EVIL PEOPLE; THOSE WHO PROFIT AND PROPHET FROM DEATH TAKE ME FROM THE TRUTH I KNOW; GOD FOR WHOM I CALL LOVEY FROM TIME TO TIME; WELL, MORE TIME.</u>

LOVEY IS TRULY PRECIOUS TO ME AND I CANNOT LET EVIL PEOPLE KILL ME.

Evil People do not tell you of the consequence of 1 Sin.

Evil People do not tell you the truth of God because; what they say is the truth, and what they are doing is God's Work. But what Evil People do not tell you is, which God they work for. <u>Nor do we as humans ask these people that profess to be of God; WHAT GOD THEY WORK FOR, SERVE, PROTECT, BOW DOWN TO, AND MORE?</u>

So as evil is guilty, we as humans are also guilty of being mislead.

Absolutely no one can be of God and give you all that is unclean to eat, drink, read, think, live by, live in, commune in, sleep in, die in, baptize in, and more. Thus know, <u>**baptism is of Death and not Life.**</u>

Baptism do not cleanse you of your sins.

Baptism do not cleanse your Spirit.

Baptism do not clear your Sin Record which is your Death Record.

Baptism do not bring you closer to God.

Baptism do not take your spirit out of Hell if your Spirit is in Hell or Hell Bound.

Baptism do not save you from Hell if you have more Sins than Good.

God cannot expunge your sins for you. You have to; must ask those you've sinned against for forgiveness. And in doing so, here on Earth; it does not mean all is truly forgiven.

Spiritual Forgiveness I am going to leave alone because; <u>GOD HAS NOT EDUCATED ME FULLY AND TRULY ON SPIRITUAL FORGIVENESS.</u>

Listen, I CANNOT LET EVIL PEOPLE CONTINUE TO TAINT GOD AND DEPICT GOD AS A MONSTER.

I CANNOT LET EVIL PEOPLE CONTINUE TO TAINT GOD BY LYING ON GOD.

GOD CANNOT AND WOULD NEVER BOW DOWN TO DEATH BECAUSE, GOD DID NOT CREATE DEATH. HUMANS CREATED AND OR,

GAVE RISE TO DEATH WITH OUR SIN AND SINS. THEREFORE, DEATH HAS AND HAVE MADE EARTH ITS HOME.

Now tell me. <u>WHAT LIES HAVE GOD TOLD ON ANY HUMAN; ANYONE FOR THAT MATTER?</u>

WHAT LIES DID GOD GIVE HUMANS TO LIVE BY?

WHAT LIES DID GOD GIVE HUMANS TO SPREAD?

WHAT LIES DID GOD GIVE HUMANS TO PREACH AND TEACH?

Now tell me. <u>WHERE IS OUR RESPECT AND TRUTH FOR GOD AND OF GOD?</u>

Our life here on Earth is fueled by hate and lies. Now tell me, when did God say, <u>let's create man and fuel their life with hate and lies so that they can die; go to hell and face a more brutal death?</u>

<u>AS HUMANS WE COMMAND RESPECT YET, CANNOT RESPECT GOD.</u>

AS HUMANS WE COMMAND TRUTH YET, CANNOT TELL THE TRUTH. So now tell me. IF YOU CANNOT TELL THE TRUTH, HOW ARE YOU GOING TO LIVE BY THE TRUTH OF YOU AND GOD?

Yes, I cuss out the White Race and will forever cuss them out because of the lies they tell and spread about Life, and God. God do not deserve the lies of anyone yet, as humans we do all to destroy God and the Truth of God by, lying and spreading lies when it comes to God; Life. God did not give the White Race, or any race lies. So, why do we as humans do this; lie on God?

Right now, I truly don't want to know but I know. More volcanoes are going to erupt I know this for a fact without doubt. Earth must burn and she is burning.

Life; Earth can no longer accommodate death in her domain. All that must go, have to go. It's a must.

Humans do not want or need the protection of God or Earth and because of this. MOTHER EARTH AND GOD HAVE TO; MUST STEP ASIDE AND LET WHAT IS TO HAPPEN HAPPEN. God and Earth can no longer interfere. The time of Death is up therefore, the Death you chose and choose for self, you have to live with, and go with.

God did try. It is us as humans that have and has crucified God with our lies; the lies we tell, the lies we live in so yes, *GOD LEARNT THE HARD WAY BECAUSE; HUMANS ARE STILL TRYING TO NAIL, AND KILL GOD LIKE THEIR LYING STORY OF JESUS.*

WIN *by Kiprich*

No fi real Lovey. Humans nuh like yu.

If we as humans truly loved you, cared for you, would we not cherish you, and do all to save ourself with you in goodness and truth?

Lovey. A SUH THE CHILDREN AND PEOPLE OF DEATH HATE AND LOATHE YOU THAT THEY WOULD DO ALL TO TAKE LIFE FROM YOU?

No Lovey. YOU NEED TO PROTECT YOUR LIFE FROM HUMANS. Truly listen to GOD IS LOVE by Beres Hammond and Popcaan. Is it not evil people here on Earth that is doing all to kill You and Mother Earth?

Isn't it Evil People that are defaming your character?

Isn't it Evil People that are pushing Death?
Isn't it Evil People that put Death over Life?

Isn't it Evil People that are encouraging others to accept Death?

Isn't it Evil People; Political Leaders, and more that send their citizens on the Battlefield of Death to defy Life; take life from self, and others?

So now tell me Lovey. _Why are humans globally not seeing this; the ills and lies of the White Race of Pathological Liars including, Political Leaders, Gang Leaders, Corporate Liars, Clergies of Demonic Liars, and more?_

Why are Blacks following behind the lies of the White Race of Pathological Liars, and more?

When are we truly going to wake up?

Now Lovey. Do you want me to decipher Death's Book – Man's so-called Holy Bible for humans to see, and know the truth?

Please let me know because if so being, I will be more than happy to do so if it means _people will put down the LIES OF MEN, AND ACCEPT THE TRUTH AND GOODNESS OF LIFE; YOU._

Life is worth it Lovey, it is humans that cannot see this; THE WORTH, TRUTH, AND GOODNESS OF LIFE.

I am tired of cussing now Lovey. It's time I educate; teach a different way. I need the truth and goodness I teach to impact life in a true, great, and powerful way that it has more than a lasting effect on life here on Earth, in the Spiritual Realm, and Beyond.

I need true change for the better here on Earth Lovey.

I need true change for the better for our good and true own.

I need true change for you, me, and Mother Earth Lovey. These changes cannot be negative. These changes must be forever ever without end good, true, positive, ever growing up good and true, and more good and true things.

There is so many things happening here on Earth, and I am so going to leave it alone because; I truly need something better for self. Humans cannot continue to negatively impact Earth with their sins.

We treat Earth like a dumping ground and Earth cannot continue to let humans do this to her.

Humans respect absolutely nothing, so why should Earth or You Lovey respect humans?

Humans respect absolutely nothing, so why should You Lovey or Earth protect humans?

Lovey, who needs the nastiness of humans in the Spiritual Realm?

I certainly don't, and I know you don't either Lovey come on now. Is this not why THE SPIRITUAL AND THE PHYSICAL IS/ARE SEPARATED?

Is Creation not truly separated from Procreation?

Michelle

My muscles – nerves is so not right right now, but I am so not going to worry about my body. I did not get optimal sleep last night. This is fine but body wise, so not fine for me.

Dream world wow to what I am seeing.

I truly do not know why the owner – dead owner to G98.7 is trying to reach out to me, but he cannot reach me. He is not being allowed to reach me. So yes, something is truly not right somewhere with him and or, his radio station. And I am going to leave things alone because, I truly do not know what he needs from me for him not to be resting in peace.

Dreamt Dan Dan. She got married and changed her name in her passport to reflect her new name. Oh man; I cannot tell you the name because, I forgot it. She also showed me the name in her Canadian Passport, but the name was handwritten. She had taken her passport to the Passport Office to change it, and they changed it right there and then for her. I was worried about the validity of the passport because, it her name was handwritten, and no stamp was in the passport to signify that the Passport Office had changed her name. Though her name was changed in the passport, the name I saw did not reflect her new name.

So yes, death is coming. I do not know who in Dan Dan's family is going to pass on. I will find out eventually and let you know. And yes, it's more than one person that is going to die.

Now this dream was before my Dan Dan dream.

Dreamt I was somewhere. Someone was trying to cover up something. There were artifacts and money hidden. Drugs and or, narcotics was also used because you could see the packets and or, packages of narcotics. Dead bodies were all around. You could see the dead bodies. This one girl that looked Babylonian with Black Hair and Slender Built was shot. She was not dead but she was lying on the floor as if dead but she was not dead.

From the looks of it; the scene, a sting operation had gone wrong because this guy was shot in the process. I could not see his face, all I saw was cops; this one police officer female came in. She had a badge – police badge in her hand. Then scene for me got foggy. I could hardly see all but, I did see when she held on to his; her colleague's hand. They were looking for him. Now, they found him and rescued him; their colleague.

After that I was in Kenya and all you saw was American Soldiers marching and or, walking. They were not in green but an orangey uniform without helmet. All the soldiers were White Males.

Was I perturbed in the dream that American Soldiers were in Kenya?

Yes

Therefore, I truly do not know what Coup is going to take control of an African Land to see the United States Army involved.

You know what. Let me forget it and not speculate because my temper is flaring right now to see THE DISGUSTING WAY BLACKS IN AFRICA LIVE.

No, I am going to go off and cuss out Africans reckless and rude.

F AFRICANS. ESPECIALLY BLACK AFRICANS ON A WHOLE TO THE WAY THEY ARE LIKE WORSE THAN THE SCUMS OF THE EARTH TO THE WAY THEY TREAT THEIR OWN.

LITERALLY BUN UNNU. UNNU WUS DAN HOGS.

No. HOW THE F CAN ANYONE OF YOU CALL YOURSELVES BLACK? NOT ONE OF YOU KNOW WHAT IT MEANS TO BE BLACK. YOU'RE ALL FRAUDS. NO WONDER AFRICA IS THE WAY IT IS. DI BC WEEPING WILLOW OF THE WORLD. PEOPLE CAN COME INTO AFRICA AND USE THE LOTS OF YOU LIKE BITCHES; YES, SHIT AND UNNU HAFFI SUCK THE SHIT WEY UNNU GET.

Yes, all of Africa can hate my ass now, I truly do not care or give a damn. YOU'RE ALL A DISGRACE TO BLACK LIFE PERIOD.

YOU'RE ALL THE DEVIL'S BITCHES TO THE WAY AFRICA IS. NO WONDER THE DEVIL CAN USE THE LOTS OF YOU SO AT WILL.

NOT ONE OF YOU KNOW WHAT IT IS TO BE BLACK.

WAKE THE BLEEP UP AND SEE WHAT IS GOING ON AROUND YOU.

No Lovey, coo pan dem.

No coo pan dem.

Living worse than dogs. Then you have some Blacks _HAVE THE NERVE TO SAY_

AFRICA IS WHERE ALL BLACKS COME FROM. BUN DAT LIE. NOT ALL BLACKS ORIGINATED IN AFRICA.

Yes, THE BLACK SELLS OUTS COME OUT OF AFRICA THUS, SLAVERY, AND ALL THAT IS ILL.

SATAN AND THE CHILDREN AND PEOPLE OF SATAN; DEATH HAD TO USE AFRICA. THUS, AFRICANS WERE/ARE USED TO BRAINWASH AND TAINT THE OTHER BLACKS THAT DID NOT FOLLOW IN THE FOOTSTEPS OF DEATH; EVIL.

Now tell me Lovey. WHAT MAKES AFRICANS BLACK WHEN THEY CAN'T EVEN DEFEND YOU OR TELL THE TRUTH OF YOU?

No Lovey, mek mi cuss out Africans reckless and rude.

No Lovey, MEK DEM; AFRICANS GI WI BACK WI BLACKNESS.

No Lovey, let me be a giver back taker now to how pissed I am. TAKE OUR BLACK SKIN FROM AFRICANS. TAKE ALL THE WATER, ALL THE RICHES, ALL THE BLESSINGS YOU'VE

GIVEN AFRICA; MAMA AFRICA BACK, AND LET THE WORLD SEE AND KNOW THE LIARS THEY ARE.

MEK DEM WEEP MORE NOW LOVEY COME ON NOW. EVERYTHING TAKE BACK FROM THEM; AFRICA; AFRICANS.

TAKE OUR HAIR BACK TOO. LET NONE IN AFRICA HAVE OUR BEAUTIFUL AND NATURAL NAPPY, HAPPY, AS PAPPY HAIR. THEY ARE NOT WORTHY OF YOU LOVEY OR OUR HAIR COME ON NOW.

No Lovey, HOW THE HELL CAN YOU WANT US TO GO BACK TO THE SOUTHERN LANDS OF AFRICA KNOWING THE WAY AFRICA; AFRICANS DISGRACE THEIR BLACK SKIN, BLACK CULTURE, MUSIC, HAIR, YOU LOVEY, SELF, LAND, AND MORE?

No Lovey. I NEED TO BOYCOTT ALL OF AFRICA RIGHT NOW GIVEN THE DREAM.

No Lovey. ALL THE COUPS AND BLACK LEADERS OF THE GLOBE FROM AFRICA TO THE CARIBBEAN THAT LIVE BY WHITE RULE, AND THE BULLSHIT WHITES GIVE THEM; COLONIZATION, THEIR

BRAINWASHED MENTALITY, AND MORE, BUN DI LOTS OF THEM, AND LET HELL CONSUME THEM AND LAND RIGHT NOW BY YOU WALKING AWAY FROM ALL A DEM TO THE WAY I AM UPSET.

YOU ARE BLACK LANDS. WHY DO YOU HAVE THE ARMY OF DEATH ESPECIALLY AMERICAN SOLDIERS COMING – WALKING IN YOIUR LAND AND BRINGING FORTH FURTHER CONDEMNATION AND SIN IN YOUR LAND?

No Lovey. IT'S TIME YOU FULLY WALK AWAY FROM THE ENTIRE CONTINENT OF AFRICA BECAUSE BLACKS TOO FOOL FOOL. Look at what we as Black People has and have become. From creators; advanced, and educated beings to become the dung of Earth for the different races. So yes, I am pissed right now Lovey.

No Lovey, LOOK AT HOW UNCIVILIZED BLACKS HAVE BECOME. Murdering each other to please their WHITE SLAVE MASTERS – THE DIFFERENT DEATHS.

Look at how some gangs kidnap and rape their own. Now tell me Lovey; <u>ARE THESE THE PEOPLE YOU WANT TO SAVE?</u>

<u>HAVE MOTHER AFRICA NOT HELD HER HEAD DOWN IN SHAME AND DISGRACE TO SEE WHAT HER PEOPLE HAVE AND HAS BECOME?</u> No Lovey, you cannot say no because, MAMA AFRICA YEARS AGO ASKED ME FOR PRAYER. THIS YOU CANNOT DENY AND SAY NO TO.

No Lovey, <u>WHEN DO WE AS BLACKS REPRESENT SELF AND EACH OTHER IN A POSITIVE AND TRUE WAY?</u>

AFRICANS SHOULD KNOW DEATH LOVEY COME ON NOW.

AFRICANS SHOULD KNOW BETTER AND DO BETTER.

AFRICANS SHOULD KNOW WHAT DEATH IS ALL ABOUT. THEY CLAIM TO BE ORIGINAL; OF CIVILIZATION YET, HOW CIVILIZED ARE THEY TODAY?

HOW CIVILIZED WERE THEY BACK THEN?

Now tell me; how could or can we look to Africa for the truth when Africa and Africans have and has disgraced Life?

Why live for Death?
Why give up life for Death?

Now tell me Africans and Mother Africa; was it all worth it to lose your soul and life to gain nothing – Death?

Why are you killing yourself for Death?
Why are you living Death's Way?

Why are you living the frigging White Way?

Are you White?

Now let me ask all of Africa this. WHAT HAS AND HAVE HAPPENED TO THE GOOD AND TRUE BLACK WAY OF LIFE?

Why are you and the rest of the Black Populace Globally so dysfunctional that you cannot see the life God has and have given you dwindling right before your eyes?

When did Death become better than Life?

No Lovey. *WHAT GOOD LEADERSHIP DO ANY IN AFRICA HA?*

WHAT GOOD LEADERSHIP DO ANY BLACK LEADER GLOBALLY HAVE LOVEY?

When you look at Blacks Globally Lovey, are you not ashamed to see the prostitutes we've become for the different races?

Are you not ashamed to the sell outs we've become for the different races?

Are you not ashamed to see the beggars we've become for the different races?

Are you not ashamed to see how greedy and corrupt many Blacks Globally has and have become?

Are you not ashamed to see how uncivilized Blacks has and have become?

Are you not ashamed to see how dishonest Blacks have and has become?

Are you not ashamed to see how Blacks have and has disgraced self, life, each other, land, you Lovey, and more?

Now tell me Lovey. Where is our True Black Unity?

Where is our True Black Giving of helping each other good and true?

Where is our True Black Developments?

No Lovey, look at some in the Entertainment Industry how they sell themselves thus, becoming the brothel; whorehouses for those who own them; give them contracts.

Going back to the different so-called Black Leaders because there's no true Black Leaders. WHAT GOOD LEADERSHIP OR LEADERSHIP SKILLS DO ANY HAVE LOVEY?

Do they not all bow down and kiss the ass of their Colonial Slave Masters thus, MANY BLACKS LANDS ARE CORPORATE OWNED BY OTHER NATIONS; NATIONALITIES, USED, ABUSED, RAPED AND ROBBED OF THEIR RICHES, CULTURE, ARTIFACTS, DEAD, AND MORE?

No, I am pissed this morning. _How can Black People have anything of truth and value, if we do not preserve our land, and people?_

How can Black People have anything of truth and value, if we do not value you Lovey?

How can Black People have anything of truth and value, if we do not abide by your truth and laws Lovey?

How can Black People have anything of truth and value, if we do not value ourself?

HOW CAN AFRICA SAY THEY ARE AFRICANS AND KNOW NOT THE TRUTH; DO ALL THAT IS WICKED AND EVIL TO TAKE YOU FROM THE CONTINENT OF AFRICA AS WELL AS, FROM ALL BLACK PEOPLE?

SO NOW TELL ME LOVEY. _WHERE IS THE TRUE BEGINNING OF THE BLACK RACE BECAUSE IT IS TRULY NOT AFRICA?_

I AM COMPLAINING AND YES, CASTING TRUE DOUBT ON AFRICAN ORIGINS BECAUSE THESE FRAUDS ARE NOT TRUE BLACKS AS FAR AS I AM CONCERNED.

THESE FRAUDS ARE NOT OF LIFE; YOU LOVEY COME ON NOW. And no, I will not take this back.

THESE FRAUDS TRUE LIFE DID NOT COME OUT OF. THEY ARE SATAN'S OWN BECAUSE THEY UPHOLD DEATH.

And Lovey, I truly don't care if Mother Africa is upset at me because; I will not hesitate to call her a Slut, whore, and Bitch to my anger. Nastiness did come from her LOINS hence, her lying people that STOLE LIFE; THE ORIGINS AND LIFE OF TRUTH; THE TRUE AFRICANS – YES, CREATION.

No Lovey, NOT ONE IN AFRICA CAN TELL ME OR YOU, OR THE WORLD OF CREATION. SO, TELL ME, HOW THE HELL CAN THEY CALL THEMSELVES ORIGINAL WHEN THEY DON'T KNOW WHAT ORIGINAL IS?

No Lovey, coo pan dem.

If you are original and know the truth SPEAK THE TRUTH.

WALK AWAY FROM EVIL.

DO NOT LET DEATH CONSUME AFRICA.
DO NOT LET DEATH CONSUME AFRICANS.

DO NOT LET THE WORLD INCLUDING ME CAST DOUBT ON AFRICA.

DO NOT LET THE WORLD TEK AFRICANS FI PUPPUNENNAY COME ON NOW.

If you were original why the different tribes in Africa? Why the tribal warfare?

Why split up Africa into different countries; nations?

Why have different cultures? Should not your culture and heritage all be the same?

No Lovey, I am pissed.

Why the different gods in Africa if you are all original?

Why the different languages and clothing if you were all original?

No Lovey, di piss pot knowledge wey dem gi di world. No, cool your temper Michelle.

Cool your temper.

No Lovey, <u>*YOU NOA AFRICA?*</u>

Lovey, yu ha sin mek yu ha compassion for the compassionless?

Dem caane defen yu, yet yu ha compassion fi dem!!!!

Yes, Lovey I am questioning your logic this morning due to anger and my dream.

<u>*Did not MANY IN AFRICA SELL OUT THE BLACK WAY FOR THE BABYLONIAN – DEVIL'S WAY?*</u>

<u>*HAVE AFREICANS NOT BECOME THEIR OWN ENEMIES?*</u>

So now tell me Lovey. <u>*Why the hell should I feed my enemies?*</u>

<u>*Why the hell should I feed your enemies?*</u>

<u>*None in Africa can defend you Lovey. So, why feed and save them?*</u>

Have Africans not shown you Lovey they are your enemies, and true enemies?

So now tell me Lovey. Can a man; anyone forget their truth when it comes to the Truth of Life; You Lovey?

Come on let's be real here Lovey.

If Africans were true, they would never forget You; their own Good and True Black God period.

No Lovey. WHERE IS BLACK AFRICA?

Yes, I went there.

Yes, I know you are angry at me now for asking you *WHERE IS BLACK AFRICA,* but to my anger Lovey, I truly don't care if you are upset at me right now. It's time BLACK PEOPLE WAKE UP AND START LIVING RIGHT.

IT'S TIME BLACK PEOPLE BREAK AWAY FROM THE ROOT AND SINS OF EVIL; DEATH.

No Lovey. BLACK PEOPLE CANNOT CONTINUE TO LIVE THE WAY WE ARE LIVING. WE ARE DYING.

THERE IS A SPIRITUAL DEATH TO BE HAD
SO WHY ARE WE DYING TO DIE COME ON
NOW?

No Lovey. *WE ARE THE ROOT OF OUR*
PROBLEMS AS WELL.

Lovey, we cannot say we are Black and treat each other including, our land like wastelands.

We cannot say we are Black, and treat you Lovey with utter disrespect.

We cannot say we are Black, and continually invite the Children and People of Death into our land and lands. When we continue to do this, we will never get rid of the Sins and Evils that plague us and kill us.

No Lovey, we as Black People can no longer take on the Sin and Sins of our enemies come on now.

Blacks have a true culture.
Blacks have a true history.
Blacks have a true life.

Blacks have a good and true way of life.

Blacks have a true God; You Lovey come on now.

No Lovey. WHY DO WE CONTINUALLY THROW YOU AWAY FOR NAUGHT?

No Lovey. NO RELIGION SHOULD BE IN AFRICA.

You are original beings; from the beginning. Africa you say is where ALL LIFE CAME FROM. SO WHY DOES AFRICA HAVE DIFFERENT RELIGIONS?

WHY DOES AFRICA NOT HAVE LIFE?
WHY DOES AFRICA NOT CARRY LIFE?
WHY CAN'T AFRICANS LIVE LIFE?

WHY DOES AFRICA AND OR, AFRICANS CARRY THE LIES OF DEATH?

WHY DO AFRICANS SELL DEATH AND HAVE BECOME DEATH?

WHY DO AFRICANS NOT SPEAK OF YOU LOVEY; THE GOD OF LIFE; OUR LIFE?

No Lovey, WHY DO AFRICANS NOT SPEAK OF YOU, THE GOD OF LIFE; OUR LIFE?

WHY DO AFRICANS DENOUNCE YOU LOVEY?

No, they are original. WHY DENOUNCE YOUR BLACK GOD FOR DEATH?

WHY BRING DEATH INTO AFRICA?

WHY DESTROY LAND AND PEOPLE?

WHY SIDE WITH DEATH AGAINST LIFE; OUR TRUE BLACK GOD THAT GAVE US LIFE, ALL THE WEALTH; RICHES OF EARTH AND THE SPIRITUAL REALM?

WHY HAVE DIFFERENT LANGUAGES?

No Lovey, at times you spoil me, but living in the land I am in, and feeling so much pain and you look at Blacks in warm lands that can go in their backyard and pick a mango, an apple, coconut, breadfruit, plant food, go to the river, ocean, or sea to get food, I can only envy because; they have truth and beauty and destroy that truth and beauty because, they cannot be satisfied due to greed; wanting what the next person has. What belongs to person X is for person X. It is not yours come on now.

Come on Lovey. Many cannot see the truth and beauty of their land and none of you dare come at me with the land I am living in. It's time we as Black People start keeping our Black Lands, and Home safe and clean.

Look how much Death is in Black Lands Lovey.

Look at how many are living in abject poverty.

Look at how many that cannot get medical care or proper education <u>despite having the resources we need naturally to save and cure us of all ailments in our land and lands.</u>

How many put their life and beliefs in Modern Medicine Lovey?

How many has and have abandoned the Organic Way of Life?

<u>Lovey, EVERYTHING GOOD AND TRUE YOU GAVE TO THE BLACK RACE YET, WE ABANDON OUR TRUTHS AND VALUES TO BECOME SICK; SCAPEGOATS AND GUINEA PIGS FOR THOSE WHO USE AND KILL; BENEFIT OFF DEATH HERE ON EARTH.</u>

Look at how many that have and has become slaves to men, and the nastiness of men.

The way Blacks are living was and is not your Way of Life Lovey come on now. No Black Person whether living or dead can step to me and tell me _NASTINESS IS THE WAY OF LIFE OR YOUR WAY OF LIFE LOVEY._

YOU LOVEY DID NOT GIVE BLACK PEOPLE NASTY.

YOU LOVEY DID NOT GIVE AFRICANS NASTY.

YOU LOVEY DO NOT GIVE NASTY.

YOU LOVEY DID NOT CHEAT ON BLACK PEOPLE. BLACK PEOPLE CHEATED ON YOU THUS, MANY DID FORFEIT THEIR LIFE WITH YOU.

No, many will not like the truth just like White People and all of Babylon, but Bleep them all. The truth have to be; must be told.

People want saving but are not willing to change their dirty linen of self.

<u>People want saving yet, expect you Lovey to be their bitch while they go on whoring, and defile life.</u>

No, this bullshit stops now. You and Mother Earth have to put a stop to the nonsense and destruction of humans. You and Mother Earth are not humanities bitch period.

Lovey, yes, I know not all want goodness for self because; <u>*THEY TRULY CANNOT SEE THE GOODNESS THEY HAVE.*</u> Many when they get, they show off on what they have.

Lovey, look how I crave and yearn to leave this land for someplace warm where I can plant and live off the land with you and Mother Earth.

Look how I bug you and Mother Earth for clean drinking water; a true and clean home.

Lovey, look how I want to see the beauty of you with me here on Earth. The yearning and craving is there and some people have this yet, taint you and land for what; greed!!!!!!!!!!!!!

Yes, you want to live the way you want to live, and you are doing it. This is you, but do not call out to Lovey for help when all goes wrong. You cannot live right, stay not living right and leave my truth and baby; Lovey alone. Get period. And please don't be angry at me Lovey, _but I am truly tired of the UNCLEAN WAY BLACKS ARE LIVING._

I AM TIRED OF BLACKS NOT SEEING THAT THE WHITE WAY IS THE SINFUL AND DIRTY WAY.

SINS COME AT A COST TO YOUR PHYSICAL AND SPIRITUAL LIFE. THEREFORE, BLACKS NEED TO WAKE UP AND START LIVING RIGHT, AND DOING THINGS RIGHT COME ON NOW.

DEATH IS BRUTAL LOVEY COME ON NOW.
WHY LIVE TO DIE A BRUTAL DEATH?
WHY LIVE TO DIE?

Do people not know the implications of Death; SPRITUAL DEATH?

Yes, my temper is waning therefore, truly forgive me for my anger Lovey. _You know how I feel about DEATH; THE ARMIES OF DEATH._

I TRULY DO NOT KNOW WHY BLACK PEOPLE HAVE TO LIVE SO DIVIDED?

I TRULY DO NOT KNOW WHY BLACK LANDS HAVE TO BRING THE DIFFERENT ARMIES OF DEATH INTO THEIR LAND.

WHY VIOLATE YOUR LIFE AND LAND LIKE THIS?

Lovey, THE WHITE MAN CANNOT SOLVE BLACK ISSUES. WE AS BLACK PEOPLE HAVE TO SOLVE OUR OWN ISSUES. This is why we have you Lovey come on now. You are there for us, it is us as Black People that has and have forgotten. And yes, many truly do not want to know because, the dirty life they are living suit them just fine.

WE AS BLACK PEOPLE HAVE TO; NEED TO GET BACK TO THE TRUTH OF LIFE AND START LIVING GOOD AND TRUE.

WHITE GOVERNANCE IS TRULY NOT BLACK GOVERNANCE THEREFORE, THE WHITE RACE CANNOT TELL BLACK PEOPLE AND BLACK LANDS HOW TO LIVE BECAUSE, WHITES; WHITE PEOPLE TRULY DO NOT KNOW HOW TO LIVE. THEY ARE

<u>TOO PRIMITIVE KNOWLEDGE WISE COME ON NOW. And no, I am not stereotyping.</u> Whites are Primitive compared to the knowledge many in the Black Race have, know, and can do.

No Lovey, do you think if I had my own country and or, land with you, evil can cum bout dem want a place to set up shop in our lands?

Do you think if I had my own country and or, land I would sell you out Lovey?

Hell, and Death don't know me because; I AM SETTING THE FOUNDATION OF TRUTH AND GOODNESS FOR US AND OUR GOOD AND TRUE OWN.

<u>JUST AS HOW EVIL CANNOT ENTER YOUR REALM IN THE SPIRITUAL REALM LOVEY, NO FORM OF EVIL CAN ENTER OUR DOMAIN HERE ON EARTH EVER AGAIN.</u>

<u>Lovey, come on. YOU HAVE TO BE MY MORE THAN SECURITY GUARD. YOUR TRUTH AND PRESENCE MUST REPEL ALL FACETS OF EVIL COME ON NOW.</u>

Now tell me something Lovey. What is wrong with us as Black People that we want and need to die suh?

No Lovey, YOU GAVE NONE IN AFRICA DIVISION.

LOVEY, LOOK AT THE WEALTH AND ABUNDANCE OF FOOD AND WATER YOU GAVE BLACK PEOPLE AND WHAT ARE WE DOING TO IT, AND WITH IT?

ALL WI DU A SQUANDER IT ALL DEN COMPLAIN TO YU FI MORE.

Preservation come on now.

No Lovey, I cannot comprehend or overstand Black People. IF YOU WERE OUR ONE AND ONLY – TRUTH LOVEY, WE WOULD NOT BE THIS WAY.

YES, DYSFUNCTIONAL GLOBALLY.

How can we fight for our rights <u>*WHEN WE KNOW NOT WHAT OUR RIGHTS ARE?*</u>

What sense do we make in all of this?

LOVEY, HOW MANY KNOW OF YOU?
HOW MANY CAN DEFEND YOU?
HOW MANY CAN LIVE WITH YOU?

HOW MANY CAN LIVE BY THE LAW AND LAWS OF LIFE?

THE REALITY IS LOVEY:

BLACKS, ESPECIALLY BLACK AFRICANS; SOLD YOU OUT JUST LIKE THEY SOLD SOME OF THEIR OWN INTO SLAVERY TO BECOME THE BITCHES AND SCAPEGOATS OF DEATH'S CHILDREN AND PEOPLE. And I will not take those words back Lovey because you know they are true.

You gave Black People Life, and instead of keeping our life good and true, we gave it up for a home and place in hell. Yes, it's sad but this is the choice of hundreds of millions if not billions of Blacks Worldwide.

Now tell me Lovey. Why is none in the Black Race finding out that the **GRASS IS TRULY NOT GREENER ON THE OTHER SIDE?**

Let me ask you this Black People.

DO YOU KNOW WHY YOU ARE DYING GLOBALLY?

DO YOU KNOW THE TRUTH OF YOU; BLACK PEOPLE?

DO YOU KNOW YOUR TRUE ORIGINS?

DO YOU EVEN KNOW THAT GOD IS BLACK?

No, not Jesus; but the True and Living God.

As a Black Person, do you know what you are capable of in life?

Listen to me this morning, forget Africa and African Lies. Go to God for the truth of all. Yes, the Southern Lands of Africa is there, but today, I can't with Africa and Africans. My anger is getting the best of me, and it did to so far.

As Black People we cannot give up our Blackness; Black God then think all is well. All is not well. *WHEN WE GIVE UP OUR BLACK GOD, THEN THAT'S IT. GOD IS GONE. THERE IS NO RETURN.* This all in the Black Community fail to realize. God has and have stepped aside from us.

Why do you think we can't find God?

Now, I am going to go back to this song.

TAKE ME TO THE KING by Tamela Mann

HOW LONG HAVE WE AS BLACK PEOPLE BEEN TRYING TO FIND GOD?

HOW MANY OF YOU HAVE AND HAS LOST YOUR WAY?

HOW MANY OF YOU GAVE UP TRYING?

HOW MANY OF YOU HAVE AND HAS LOST HOPE?

HOW MANY OF YOU SAY F GOD, THERE IS NO GOD?

HOW MANY OF YOU CRY DAY IN AND DAY OUT AND STILL YOU HAVE NO HOPE AND RESCUE?

HOW MANY OF YOU HAVE DIED IN VAIN?

No, HOW MANY OF YOU HAVE DIED IN VAIN?

Yes, I can ask the dead that question because, none of you know Death or the Dead like I do.

God is letting the god and gods you left God for do all unto you that you desired. Life – your life was not worth it to you.

God did try with us, now look at how we have and has failed God.

Look at how we are still failing God.

Until we know the truth and go back to living by the truth, Blacks will forever die.

Blacks will forever ever fill up hell.
Blacks will forever ever not have life.
Blacks will forever ever forfeit life.

And, go there with me and your Jesus bout; Jesus died to save you let me school you. Now let me ask you this.

IF JESUS DIED TO SAVE YOU. HOW COME THERE IS SO MANY BLACK PEOPLE IN HELL?

WHY ARE BLACK PEOPLE STILL DYING?

HOW COME BLACK PEOPLE DON'T RESPECT THEIR BLACK GOD – WELL JESUS THAT DIED TO SAVE YOU?

WHY BAPTIZE AND GO BACK TO YOUR OLD WAYS?

WHY BAPTIZE AT ALL?

You are supposed to be clean, _SO, WHY ARE YOU; ALL NOT LIVING CLEAN?_

WHY IS DEATH STILL PLAGUING EARTH, AND THE PEOPLE OF EARTH?

No, truly don't come to me with nonsense. BLACK PEOPLE GAVE UP ALL THEY HAD AND HAVE INCLUDING THEIR LIFE FOR FOOLS GOLD. There are no ands, ifs, or buts about this. We did wrong.

WE TOOK THE BAIT OF DEATH AND DIED. WE ARE STILL DYING AND GOING TO DIE MORE. Hence, I tell you:

"HELL IS FULL OF BLACK PEOPLE AND RECRUITING MORE."

So yes, I cannot comprehend WHY AFRICANS WOULD DISRESPECT THEIR ORIGINS SO.

I cannot comprehend WHY AFRICANS WOULD GIVE UP THEIR BLACK GOD SO EASILY FOR DEATH.

I cannot comprehend WHY AFRICANS WOULD NOT DEFEND THEIR BLACK GOD AND KEEP LOVEY GOOD AND TRUE?

<u>HOW CAN WE AS BLACK PEOPLE SAY WE ARE ORIGINAL WHEN WE OF OURSELVES DO NOT KNOW OUR ORIGINS?</u>

Yes, many want to connect to Mama Africa, but connect to what?

What connections do all Blacks have to Africa when not all Blacks came from Africa?

The origins of Blacks did not all come from Africa because Blacks resided in other lands; were born in other lands. And this has absolutely nothing to do with MIGRATION. Therefore, Africans need to tell the truth.

Africans need to tell the truth of HOW WHITE PEOPLE CAME ABOUT.

Africans need to tell the truth of the Great Rift; Shift long before your so-called beginning; well, Adam and Eve of your bible that you know.

Now let me ask you this. Why fight for Africa when you know not what you are fighting for?

If Africa; Africans kept the truth then yes, but as it is, AFRICANS CANNOT SPEAK THE TRUTH, OR TELL YOU THE TRUTH. So now tell me, <u>WHAT GOOD CONNECTIONS CAN YOU HAVE WITH AFRICA IF ALL YOU KNOW, AND ALL YOU ARE GIVEN ARE/IS LIES.</u>

<u>Absolutely no one can find the TRUTH OF GOD IF ALL THEY ARE GIVEN IS/ARE LIES.</u>

So, know tell me. <u>How can we find the Glory of God when not one of us know what the GLORY OF GOD IS?</u>

So yes, as Black People, many things we do makes absolutely no sense to me whatsoever.

Right now. WHAT ARE WE DEFENDING?

WHY ARE WE DEFENDING DEATH?
WHY DO WE KILL OURSELVES?

WHY DO WE HATE OURSELVES SO?

<u>IS GOD NOT WORTH IT TO US?</u>
<u>IS LIFE NOT WORITH IT TO US?</u>

It's time for us as Black People to give up Death.

It's time for us as Black People to live.

As Blacks, _we cannot rely on AFRICANS TO TELL THE TRUTH BECAUSE; THEY KNOW NOT THE TRUTH, NOR ARE THEY TRUTHFUL._ IF THEY WERE, THEY WOULD NOT HIDE THE TRUTH OF LIFE, AND GOD FROM US.

No, God do not hide life from anyone yet, you have those that would rather carry the lies of death, and hand these lies down from generation to generation so that you die; Death can have life. Meaning, Death can live longer.

Now Africa.

YOU SAY YOU ARE ORIGINAL BEINGS. NOW TELL ME. _WHAT BIBLE DID GOD GIVE TO ALL OF AFRICA; ALL BLACK PEOPLE TO LIVE BY?_

No, it's not whoa. I went there.

YOU ARE ORIGINAL BEINGS. WHERE IS GOD'S BIBLE; BOOK THAT HE GOD GAVE TO ALL AFRICANS TO LIVE BY?

No Lovey, don't because; I intend to defend you to the fullest.

WHERE IS GOD'S BOOK AFRICA?
WHERE IS GOD'S BOOK OF LAWS?

WHAT BOOK DID GOD GIVE YOU TO LIVE BY AS WELL AS, ENSURE YOUR CHILDREN AND FUTURE GENERATIONS LIVE BY?

Yes, I am going there. And any of you come to me with the different Bibles of Men come and let me lock your asses further in hell with your condemned book of sin and destruction; whoredom and lies.

COME ON AFRICANS TELL ME, BECAUSE I AM CHALLENGING THE LOTS OF YOU BEFORE, GOD, MOTHER AFRICA, MOTHER EARTH, DEATH, MAN – ALL OF HUMANITY; ALL. WHAT IS GOD'S LANGUAGE SINCE THE LOTS OF YOU ARE ORIGINAL AND ALL LIFE CAME FROM AFRICA?

WHAT IS THE LANGUAGE OF GOD, BECAUSE I AM DEFENDING MY BLACK GOD, THE TRUE AND LIVING GOD THAT CREATED IT ALL?

No Lovey, let me lift you up and put you to the side, because I am questioning the validity, life, and integrity of every African globally no matter the descent.

No Lovey, don't smile because; I am deadly serious.

You take a break because none in Africa can speak and or, tell the truth.

No Lovey, EVERY AFRICAN SHOULD BE ASHAMED OF SELF AND THE LIES THEY CARRY AND CONTINUE TO CARRY AND TELL FOR DEATH, AND THE CHILDREN AND PEOPLE OF DEATH.

Therefore, Lovey I will ask you this:

HOW TRUSTWORTHY ARE ANY AFRICANS?

No Lovey. CAN YOU EVEN TRUST AFRICANS?

Yes, I will question their integrity yet again.

No Lovey, *WHAT DOES IT MEAN TO BE BLACK WHEN IT COMES TO ANY AFRICAN GLOBALLY?*

So now tell me Lovey. <u>HOW CAN WE HAVE ANY BLACK RIGHTS WHEN WE DON'T EVEN HAVE A BLACK GOD; YOU?</u>

<u>WE CAN'T EVEN BE TRUE TO YOU IN ALL THAT WE DO.</u> So why the hell should you stand with humans, and give humans a home with you when; not one can be true or truly devoted to you Lovey?

We discredit and dishonour you Lovey then have the nerve; gaul to want you to save us from Death.

<u>Where is your defence in humans Lovey?</u>

<u>Where?</u>

We slaughter your character.
We slaughter your truth.
We slaughter our life.
We slaughter Earth.

We slaughter everything then expect to be saved.

How does that work?

<u>As Black People STAND UP FOR YOUR BLACK GOD.</u> Break away from the lies the Children and

People of Death tell because; <u>DEATH IS NOT JUST</u> <u>WHITE, DEATH IS BLACK ALSO.</u> Thus, Physical and Spiritual Death.

How can we say we are Black, <u>AND DEFEND THE LIES OF DEATH?</u>

How can we say we are Black, <u>and not defend OUR BLACK RIGHTS WITH GOD?</u>

How can we say we are Black, <u>and not defend OUR BLACK LIFE WITH GOD?</u>

How can we say we are Black, <u>and not KEEP OUR LIFE AND RIGHTS; TRUTHS WITH GOD?</u>

How can we say we are Black, <u>and not INVEST SOME OF OUR GOODNESS IN GOD?</u>

How can we say we are Black, <u>AND LIVE IN DYSFUNCTION?</u>

We are not dysfunctional people yet, we live this way; in dysfunction.

How can we say we are Black, <u>and not GIVE GOD SOME OF OUR GOODNESS?</u>

How can we say we are Black, *and not* SAVE OUR BLACK GOD; LOVEY?

How can we say we are Black, *and LET* OTHER NATIONS ASSASSINATE THE CHARACTER, TRUTH, VALIDITY, LIFE, AND MORE OF OUR BLACK GOD?

How can we say we are Black, *and NOT* LIVE OUR LIFE GOOD AND TRUE THE BLACK WAY; RIGHT AND PROPER WAY?

God gave us a good and true way to live, and we allowed others to come in and dirty us; why?

Dirty cannot be clean.

Africa did taint herself long ago.
Africa did let evil into her land.
Africa did procreate with evil.
Africa did disobey God.
Africa did divorce God.

Now look at Africa.
Look at Black People on a whole.

BLACKS ARE FIGHTING BUT FIGHTING FOR WHAT?

YOU CANNOT FIGHT TO GET INCLUDED IN THE DEVIL'S SYSTEMS OF LIFE. IT MAKES ABSOLUTELY NO SENSE. <u>You are Black not White.</u>

WHY FIGHT TO BE INCLUDED IN DEATH? WHY FIGHT TO GO TO HELL?

WHY WANT AND NEED DEATH FOR SELF?

<u>*"THE WAGES OF SIN IS DEATH."*</u>

Now tell me, <u>*WHY ARE YOU PAYING DEATH TO KILL YOU?*</u>

And on this note I am going to leave off. I need to make something to eat as well as, walk my dog.

I also have to nip this man in the bud. Meaning, I cannot let this conversation I am having with him get too far. He wants a relationship with me, and I truly do not want or need one despite me telling him we can only talk as friends.

Do not insert yourself in someone's life that truly do not want or need you to be in their life. Yes, it's weird and gross for me that someone can do that. Insert their life in your life without properly knowing them. But then humans are weird. I am to a certain degree.

Friendship is friendship to me.

True friends are bliss to me. And if I only want friendship from you, I cannot hold you true or dear to me. You are just there. So yes, I have to nip this man in the bud because he truly do not get it. I do not want to be disrespectful or hurtful, but I am going to have to tell him again.

It's weird because he wants to have coffee with me and walk my dog with me, but that I can't even do. I don't want him buying me a coffee. For me, taking a coffee from him would be like taking on his darkness and I cannot do that. I refuse to take on a man's darkness or the darkness of anyone.

It's funny I wanted to make of Book of Death. No, not Bible, but a book taking about Death the right way, but I do not know what to put in that book other than what I've put in these books.

Oh man, I don't want to give you my email address for you to ask me questions about death, and what I should write about when it comes to death. Yes, in some of my earlier books; years ago, I included my email address, but that's a task for you to find now, considering the amount of books I've written over the years. So, do not task yourself in finding me this way. Hey, some of you might already know me without knowing. Hey you never know.

Listen, the Moon is back lighting up my room. And it's beautiful to see the light of the Moon dancing on my wall. So yes, I have to stay protected and safe.

Still seeing faces before me when I close my eyes, but I am not going to worry about these faces; black faces and or, faces of Black People. Hopefully, it will get to the point where I can describe the faces that I see in detail. Maybe you will know some of these people that are going to die.

So, until later or another day.

Have a truly wonderful and blessed day.

Michelle
May 30, 2021

Now let me ask you this Lovey.

As Africans, why would you want your people to die?

Why would you give your people lies to live by?

Why would you continue to trap your people and those of the Western Hemisphere in hell with your lies?

IF YOU WERE TRUE BLACKS AND TRUE TO THE BLACK RACE; WOULD YOU NOT TELL THE TRUTH, KEEP THE TRUTH, DO ALL TO SAVE THE BLACK RACE, DO ALL FOR BLACKS TO WALK IN TRUTH, TALK IN TRUTH, LIVE IN TRUTH, AND PUT DOWN ALL THAT IS OF EVIL AND DEATH?

WHY LEAD YOUR OWN ASTRAY?

WHY MISLEAD YOUR OWN?

WHY LET THE WHITE RACE MISLEAD, AND CHEAT YOUR OWN NOT JUST IN AFRICA BUT GLOBALLY?

Look how those of the Caribbean look up to Africa yet, Africa cannot help us in a positive way to break down, and get rid of the chains of Death.

TELL BLACKS THE WHITE MAN'S BIBLE IS NOT OF GOD.

TELL BLACKS THE WHITE MAN'S BIBLE IS OF DEATH BECAUSE, IT IS UNCLEAN AS WELL AS, DEFY THE LAW AND LAWS OF LIFE – GOD.

TELL BLACKS THE PROPHETS OF THE WHITE MAN'S BIBLE ARE NOT US AS A RACE AND PEOPLE. GOD WOULD NOT GIVE US LAWS TO LIVE BY AND BREAK HIS OWN LAWS BY TELLING HIS PROPHETS TO STEAL AND KILL.

TELL BLACKS THE TWELVE TRIBES OF ISRAEL IS NOT OF THE BLACK RACE BECAUSE, GOD WOULD NEVER DIVIDE HIS AND HER PEOPLE INTO TRIBES.

TELL BLACKS THAT GOD WOULD NOT LET US GO INTO UNCLEAN PLACES.

TELL BLACKS THE TRUTH OF CREATION.

TELL   BLACKS   THE   TRUTH   OF PROCREATION.

TELL BLACKS THE TRUTH OF JESUS AND MARY.

TELL BLACKS JESUS IS DEATH BECAUSE, GOD WOULD NOT LET HIS AND HER CHILDREN DIE TO SAVE DEATH'S WICKED AND EVIL OWN.

No Lovey, WHY IS IT THAT AFRICANS KEEP AFRICA TIED TO DEATH?

Divorce Death. You can.

Lovey, WHY DO BLACK PEOPLE HAVE TO SEEK DEATH.

WHY DO BLACK PEOPLE HAVE TO LIVE BY DEATH?

Do not seek death.
Do not seek the devil.
Do not seek evil.

Live come on now.

Aye Lovey. How do we save our Black Own?

How do we break the chains of death for us to see life?

How do we take the veil of death from around Blacks Globally?

Lovey, why can't Black People wake up and see and know the truth?

Now tell me. *HOW CAN WE SAY GOD, AND TRULY DO NOT KNOW YOU?*

HOW CAN WE SAY GOD, AND KEEP THE LIES OF DEATH?

HOW CAN WE SAY GOD, AND CONTINUE TO PRAISE AND WORSHIP DEATH?

HOW CAN WE SAY GOD, AND NOT WANT AND NEED LIFE; TO LIVE?

HOW CAN WE SAY GOD, AND NOT LIVE LIFE GOOD AND TRUE?

HOW CAN WE SAY GOD, AND TEACH WRONG?

HOW CAN WE SAY GOD, AND PRAY WRONG?

HOW CAN WE SAY GOD YET, TELL LIES ON YOU LOVEY?

HOW CAN WE SAY GOD YET, WANT TO RETURN HOME IN LIES?

Now tell me. HOME TO WHERE LOVEY?

YOU CANNOT RECEIVE PEOPLE THAT DO NOT KNOW YOU.

YOU CANNOT RECEIVE PEOPLE THAT ACCEPT LIES WHEN IT COMES TO YOU.

YOU CANNOT RECEIVE PEOPLE THAT BELIEVE IN LIES ABOUT YOU.

YOU CANNOT RECEIVE PEOPLE THAT TELL LIES ON YOU.

YOU CANNOT RECEIVE PEOPLE THAT PRAISE DEATH.

YOU CANNOT RECEIVE PEOPLE THAT PREACH LIES WHEN IT COMES TO YOU.

YOU CANNOT RECEIVE PEOPLE THAT BELIEVE IN TRIBAL WARFARE.

YOU CANNOT RECEIVE PEOPLE THAT LIVE FOR DEATH AND DISHONOUR.

YOU CANNOT RECEIVE PEOPLE THAT BELIEVE IN PROPHETS.

YOU CANNOT RECEIVE PEOPLE THAT ACEEPT AND BELIEVE IN THE LIES OF THE BIBLE. AND YOU DO NOT ACCEPT THESE PEOPLE LOVEY I KNOW.

Lovey, now tell me. <u>WHAT IS SO GREAT ABOUT BONDAGE?</u>

What is so great about the bondage Blacks are living in globally?

What is so great about the lies and deceit Blacks believe in, and has and have accepted globally?

Now Lovey let me ask you this.

<u>WHY AFRICA?</u>

Why let Death take Africa?

Why let Death separate Africa into all that is unholy and unclean?

No Lovey, why were Blacks fooled so much?

Okay. I know how you've been trying to protect me. You've shown me so much. <u>Blacks do have the gift of sight SO WHY DID BLACKS OF OLD NOT KEEP THEIR GIFT OF SIGHT AND KNOWLEDGE?</u>

Yes, I know the truth. <u>IN ORDER TO DECEIVE A NATION, YOU HAVE TO USE THEIR OWN KIND. THEREFORE, EVIL INFILTRATED THEIR OWN USING THOSE WHO LOOKED LIKE US BUT WAS NOT TRULY OF US</u>. So yes, I know the answer to that which I know. But Lovey, this still do not explain why Africans did not rely on their sight. Yes, I know not all of Africa was tricked and deceived, but Lovey. How did these Blacks come about?

Something still do not add up with me.

Creation and procreation. Yes, I know many Blacks broke the LAW OF LIFE AND MARRIAGE.

It is forbidden for Clean to lay with Unclean. When Clean lay with Unclean then Life becomes hell due to the negative nature we take on. Thus; **<u>WHEN CLEAN LAY WITH</u>**

UNCLEAN WE GIVE RISE TO DEATH. *And yes, I know this is a poor explanation but in reality, I know the truth.*

So now tell me Lovey. WHY ARE WE FOOLED BY BLACKS THAT LOOK LIKE BLACKS BUT FALL UNDER THE ORDER OF DEATH?

Lovey, ARE WE THAT CLOSED MINDED TO OUR OWN BLACKS?

Yes, Michelle that was a stupid question to ask. You are a living testament and testimony to this. Is he not dark and you see him, yet you still talk to him? Now you have to nip things in the bud before things get out of hand.

So yes, we are fooled because sight not all have.

Many people cannot see the ills of their own Blacks.

You didn't until now. Now you are relying on God and your sight to see and know.

Wow Lovey because things are so different. As Black People we need to start listening.

We need to start seeing.
We need to start knowing.
We need to start sensing.

We need to start relying on God; You Lovey.

We need to start living right.
Eating right.
Singing right.
Sleeping right.
Teaching right.
Dancing right.
Chanting right.
Vibing right.

Procreating – no, creating right.

Writing right, and more good and true things.

Oh man, I did not tell you all about my tiger dream, but I know the cause of this dream.

So, as I close this book Lovey, truly hear me and continually be with me good and true.

In all you do Lovey, you need to be the foundation and strength here on Earth of our good and true only.

I need you to be my foundation and strength here on Earth not just in the Spiritual Realm.

I need you to keep undesirables at bay and away from me here on Earth. You cannot just show me people and not keep unclean people away from me.

This man I told him I do not want a relationship with him, but he insists on trying. Lovey, you are my foundation, and I truly do not want or need unclean beasts; men or women in my life. So where does the problem lie in you protecting me from unclean men; unclean all? Well, you are. I just don't want or need unclean men or women extending their line to me relationship wise or otherwise.

I need you Lovey to ordain and send me the right someone.

I need you to ordain and send me that good and clean someone.

I need you to ordain and send me that positive someone.

The one you approve good and true for me.

I truly cannot deal with relationships that are not of you and me. Relationships that are not true to life, true to us, positive, ever growing up good and true, and more.

You know me yet you are failing me. Well, I am failing me too. However, Lovey, you are my first defence of truth and goodness. So, please; do not let me meet people that are not on our level of truth and cleanliness in that way or otherwise.

Truly be my guard and safeguard all the time.

Yes, I need a relationship with someone, but not with someone who is truly not right for me and you. You have to be in the mix of my life and stay Lovey come on now.

You know my desires yet, you are limited with me Lovey why?

What do you not get when it comes to me and you, and the truth and cleanliness I require from you? Well, the both of us.

Yes, I have to go now but later we will talk.

Michelle

<u>BOOKS WRITTEN BY MICHELLE JEAN 2021</u>

MY TALK JANUARY 2021

MY TALK JANUARY 2021 – BOOK TWO

MINI BOOK

JUST TALKING – THINKING

A LITTLE TALK WITH MOTHER EARTH

I NEED ANSWERS GOD

POETRY MY WAY

THE MIND AND SPIRITUALITY

I NEED ANSWERS GOD – PART TWO

MY NIGHTS

I NEED ANSWERS GOD – PART THREE

GOD IS GOOD

WHAT ABOUT US

WOW WHAT

<u>COMING SOON</u>